RIAM
Local Centre
Exams

N.B. The following pieces can only be presented for exams in **2020** and for the **first session only in 2021**.
They **may not** be presented in 2019.

GRADE II

Candidates **must prepare any three** of the following pieces

Friedrich Burgmüller	*Innocence*	2
Ludwig van Beethoven	*Ecossaise in G*	3
Barbara Arens	*Fuzzy Wuzzy Jazzy*	4
Christian Petzold	*Minuet in G minor, BWV Anh. 115*	6
Elijah Thomas Burke	*The Chirpy Robin*	7
Robert Schumann	*Soldier's March*	8

Explore the 2019–2022 RIAM Local Centre Piano Syllabus for all exam requirements and new information including fixed deadlines, general theory section, and the check list at the start of different exam categories, all of which are explained in the introduction.

For teaching notes, updates, and information relevant to the Local Centre, please refer to the RIAM Teaching and Learning Network website: https://network.riam.ie/

Project manager: Majella Boland.
Selector and editor: Lorna Horan.
Proofing: Majella Boland, Dearbhla Brosnan, Lorna Horan, and Réamonn Keary.
Typesetter: Eneko O'Carroll Iturregui: enekoocarroll@gmail.com
Cover design: Nathan Somers: studio@nathansomersdesign.ie
Printer: Summit DPS Ltd email: info@summitdps.ie

Innocence

Friedrich Burgmüller

Ecossaise in G

Ludwig van Beethoven

Allegretto

★ Repeats are not required in the exam.

Fuzzy Wuzzy Jazzy

Barbara Arens

Minuet in G Minor

BWV Anh. 115

Christian Petzold

★ Repeats are not required in the exam.

The Chirpy Robin

Elijah Thomas Burke

Elijah Thomas Burke is the 2020 RIAM Composition Winner.

Soldier's March

Animato, alla marcia

Robert Schumann

★ **Repeats are not required in the exam.**